Hubert

St Lu and The Love of God

from Edmund.

Edmund S Haviland

The Phoenix Press
SWANSEA

Published by: The Phoenix Press (SWANSEA)
                PO Box 41, Bangor, Gwynedd
                LL57 1SB, UK

Typeset by: Paragon Typesetters, Queensferry, Clwyd

Printed by: Henry Ling Ltd., The Dorset Press,
                Dorchester

ISBN   1 85865 075 5

A CIP catalogue record for this book is available from the British Library.

CONTENTS

Cover illustration: *The Holy Family with St. Elizabeth and
Saint John the Baptist
by Peter Paul Rubens
Reproduced by permission of
The Art Institute of Chicago*

To my Be Be
who especially stimulated this
and to my Mother and Father
with love and gratitude

FOREWORD

The following study has brought together some topics which have been unresolved in my mind for some years, and which have arisen from or been stimulated by pastoral experiences. Reflection and reading in the more relaxed life of retirement has, it seems, borne some fruit.

The earliest puzzle was the relationship between forgiveness as understood by Jews in Old Testament times and that proclaimed by the early Church and by Christians subsequently. Forgiveness through Jesus Christ alone seemed to preclude any others — which conflicted with the Jewish scriptures and belief. (I have been surprised and ashamed by my calmly accepting a doctrine unreconcilable with the Jewish one, while using the Jewish psalms as a vital and valuable basis for daily public and private worship.)

Related to this I have wondered about the evidence for the strong and constant statements in the (Church of England) liturgy that God's forgiveness was dependant on both penitence and faith.

Where was the Gospel justification for

saying this? What precisely was the faith, and the degree of penitence, required? Was it true, as some Christians seemed to maintain, that a necessary pre-condition of being a disciple of Christ, or even a child of God, was the conviction that one was a sinner — in whom there was no health?

Where and how do people of other faiths in one God — or in more than one, or of no faith — stand in relation to God who is the Father of Jesus Christ? Could we possibly say or even suggest that there is no forgiveness for people who have had no chance even of hearing of Jesus?

These are not uncommon questions, yet it seems a weakness that Christians give conflicting and unclear answers.

With these and other wonderings in various parts of my mind, and with a lively attraction to and interest in the third Gospel and its unique and fascinating stories, I found further reading of St Luke rewarding and fruitful. I am grateful to various scholarly authors and some friends and relations who have stimulated and encouraged me.

Biblical quotations are from the New English Bible.

ONE

The Comings

St Luke gives his readers the great benefit of his reason for writing his Gospel. Theophilus, to whom it is addressed, is already familiar with the story of Jesus; Luke wants to be sure he is well instructed about it, so he sets chosen sections of the story in a considered and deliberate order. Theophilus and we ourselves may examine what Luke compiled, and may therefore be led to acknowledge that the message is received and understood.

Luke begins with a fascinating and vividly descriptive picture of identifiable people, named and pinpointed both historically and geographically, who have some other-worldly mystical experiences; these he relates as signs of the action of God among them. God is the God of the Hebrews, the children of Israel, whose sacred scriptures are referred to and provide a background to the events and the conversations in which the characters are involved.

The first two chapters as we have them are,

even in translation, a beautiful drama of angels and men, women and babies, ritual and work, comings and goings in town and countryside, talking and singing in prose and poetry (eminently actable by adults and children!) — all conveying important and mysterious meaning to the participants, both audience and readers alike, if they have ears to hear, eyes to see.

Jesus, the central character, then emerges, in the third and following chapters, in adulthood, and, having been established as fulfilling a uniquely divine purpose, lives a brief and clearly human life which ends in his young manhood with another mysterious drama of pathos and triumph. But the first three chapters seem to provide the introduction and to outline the significance of the whole work: yet there is, I suggest, a special first climax at the end of chapter 7.

Luke starts, then, with the conception and birth of the two boys John and Jesus; the details and experiences of their respective parents are interwoven in the narrative, so that in these stories and in those of their infancy and public appearances we are surely invited to compare and distinguish and contrast them, and so to discover what St Luke wanted Theophilus and his successors to know. A diagramatic plan of the inter-relation of the introductory stories is on the next page.

Diagram of the contents of Chapters 1, 2 & 3 of St Luke's Gospel.

Key:
Passages, with verse nos., referring to John the Baptist   – – – – – – –
                                                    to Jesus   = = = = = =

Announcement of Births   (A)   Their Circumcisions   (C)
Their Births   (B)   Baptising and Baptism (D)

Chapter 1

(A)
v5 – – – – – – 25

(B)
v1 ===

(A)
26 ================= (Magnificat) 56

36 – – – 45

(B) – – – (C) – – – (Benedictus)
57   68 ======== 75   80

Chapter 2

(No ref. to John)

(B)
v1 ===

(A)
26 ================= (C) (Presentation) (To Temple, age 12) 52

Chapter 3

(D)
v1 – – – – – – – – – 20

(D)   (Genealogy)
16,17 =================================
21   38

We notice, then, how the Gospel opens. John and Jesus are given approximately the same amount of space in overlapping sections, not as separate stories, in the first three chapters. Further examination shows striking correspondence and parallels in the events and conversations, and in the words used to describe them. These are set out in pages 6-7 following.

All these parallels must be deliberate and purposeful, yet it is strange that one story is nowadays commonly discussed without the other. For the virginal conception of Jesus is so closely related to the equally impossible, humanly speaking, conception of John: each is a surprising and significant act of God with whom "nothing shall be impossible". Luke takes great trouble to intertwine their narration. He even inserts Zechariah's prophecy, "Benedictus", between his reporting of the respective births, and therein combines "Praise to the God of Israel" for both: first for the deliverer from the house of David whose actual birth he has yet to refer to, and then for his own child, the Lord's forerunner.

What are we being told? Surely more than the bare facts would seem at first to state. If it is all literal narrative, it presents great problems, beautiful and moving though it is. It all seems so unlikely — and the two stories together! Yet nowhere else are they told or referred to. St Matthew's Gospel has Jesus's birth story but with different accompanying events.

Furthermore, Luke alone goes on to relate and apparently compare the boys' growing up and their ministries and messages, even their lives and deaths, with both similarities and contrasts.

Are not Gabriel and the angels the clue to what it is all about, and so to the true place of the stories in the whole scheme and intention of Luke's work? These are neither fairy stories nor designed for children: they are for adults; they are about the messengers of God who come to mankind with messages of deep truths, from the realms of eternity to mortals on earth, about reality and the fundamental relationships between God and man. Angels are called into play as interpreters and lively links. They appear again in Luke's story only twice: once "bringing him strength" as Jesus prayed "in anguish of spirit" to the Father on the Mount of Olives; and then on the Resurrection morning the faithful women found "two men in dazzling garments" at their side in his tomb with mysterious words of comfort in their terror.

We see from the stories that the coming of John and Jesus portrays divine action in human life. God is found to be working through people, needing their response, overcoming their fear. It is clearly his initiative, and a sign of his goodwill to all people, and all for their sake.

John the Baptist	Jesus
Birth announced Lk 1.5-25	*Birth announced Lk 1.26-38*
Elizabeth: barren	Mary: girl . . . a virgin
Zechariah her husband both of priestly descent	Joseph her betrothed descendant of David
While burning incense in the temple (in Jerusalem) angel appeared: "I am Gabriel, I am sent to speak to you"	To Nazareth in Galilee, angel Gabriel sent from God went in with a message.
He was startled . . . fearful	She was deeply troubled . . . wondered
Angel: "Do not be afraid, your prayer has been heard, Elizabeth shall bear you a son. You shall name him John"	Gabriel: "Do not be afraid, God has been gracious to you, you shall conceive and bear a son. You shall give him the name Jesus"
He will be great in the eyes of the Lord	He will be great; he will bear the title Son of the Most High
He will bring back many Israelites to the Lord God	He will be king over Israel for ever
Zechariah: "How can I be sure of this? I am an old man, and my wife is well on in years"	Mary: "How can this be? I am still a virgin"

6

John continued	Jesus continued
Gabriel: "You will lose your speech.	Gabriel: "The Holy Spirit will come upon you; (your) holy child will be called Son of God.
My words will be proved true"	God's promises will never fail"
Elizabeth: "This is the Lord's doing"	Mary: "I am the Lord's servant; as you have spoken, so be it"

[Elizabeth is visited by Mary]

Birth and Circumcision 1.57-80	*Birth and Circumcision 2.1-40*
	Mary was expecting a child . . .
The time came for Elizabeth's child to be born	The time came for her baby to be born
She gave birth to a son	She gave birth to a son
Her neighbours and relatives heard . . . were delighted	(To) Shepherds out in the fields an angel: I have good news for you — great joy coming to the whole people
On the eighth day they came to circumcise the child	Eight days later the time came to circumcise him
Elizabeth and Zechariah: His name is John	He was given the name Jesus
As the child grew up he became strong in spirit . . . The hand of the Lord was upon him	The child grew big and strong and full of wisdom . . . God's favour was upon him

7

TWO

The Contrasts

The similarities and the parallels in Luke's arrangement also serve to point up the contrasts. Zechariah and his wife Elizabeth are of priestly families, devout and socially prominent. Mary is a girl betrothed to a man called Joseph, a descendant of King David: otherwise each is quite obscure. Zechariah's son is to be like Elijah, God's forerunner possessed by his spirit to prepare people for his coming. Mary's son will be called Son of God, King over the people of God for ever.

Zechariah's John is a prophet with two commissions: to administer baptism as a sign of repentance and forgiveness to people on certain conditions, and to introduce Jesus as one who is mightier than himself and who has a superior baptism — "with the Holy Spirit". For John there is no other ministry and he has no further message; imprisonment and beheading soon follow, and he is not concerned to make disciples.

Jesus, however, is duly proclaimed "Son of God", by word and sign, at his baptism by John, and he then embarks on a lively and controversial ministry. He too proclaims forgiveness in the name of God but (as we shall notice) in a contrasting context. When his death comes, it is dramatic and public and accompanied by startling signs. His disciples are surprised by and convinced of his resurrection. They receive his command to be his witnesses to all nations. He parted from them with his blessing, and left them praising God.

It seems that Luke's purpose is to point the contrast between John and Jesus, partly by first showing the similarities in their comings. There are undoubted parallels, but in the end divergence — and in the divergence is the emphasis of the good news of and from God. John and his message die: Jesus and his message go round the world.

We may now look at the contrast for Luke in the messages of John and Jesus.

John addressed the people who came to him as a "viper's brood" and spoke of the "coming retribution" that they could reasonably expect (chapter 3.7). He proclaimed a "baptism in token of repentance for the forgiveness of sins" (3.3), and demanded that repentance be proved by the fruit it bears so as to validate his baptism (3.8). "Every tree that fails to produce fruit is cut down" (3.9) (St John's Gospel records Jesus's use of this metaphor in a

9

different context — chapter 15). Then he gave instructions and commands about how repentance was to be demonstrated.

Jesus's proclamation had no such conditions. He gave his message and his "baptism" in, of and with the Holy Spirit without requiring signs of acceptance. He often gave it, by word and action, as he met strangers for the first time: there was no question or possibility of any condition being fulfilled beforehand, nor was any consequence demanded. He did not preach God's forgiveness to sinners who were penitent but to all sinners.

For instance: a man with an unclean spirit in the synagogue at Capernaum was healed (4.33); Simon's wife's mother was healed of a fever on his visit to her home (4.38); many were cured of diseases and devils as he laid his hands on them (4.40); a man in one of the towns who was covered with leprosy was cleansed and the cure certified (5.12); similarly great crowds gathered to be cured (5.15); a paralysed man on a bed rose to his feet and took his bed home (5.17): here is also the first proclamation of forgiveness in Luke; a man's withered arm was restored (6.6); crowds were cured (6.17-19), and so was a Roman centurion's servant who was ill and near to death (7.7); many sufferers from various ailments were cured, and on many blind people he bestowed sight (7.21). All these were apparently at their first meeting with Jesus; all were unknown to him, and no questions were asked or conditions required.

Many of these incidents are the same as in Mark. There is the one notable change made by Luke (if we may agree that Luke had access to the earlier Gospel of Mark) — in altering the tense of the verb in 5.20 and 23 from the present tense to the perfect, so that Mark's "are forgiven" becomes "have been forgiven" for Luke; he does the same again in chapter 7: the significance of this will be discussed later.

These healings were to be seen (says Luke) as signs of the proclamation of God's message in action (4.18, and 7.22 to John the Baptist) apparently indiscriminately and unconditionally. Healing was a sign of God's care, love and acceptance, and of his forgiveness. The Twelve were commissioned to go and proclaim this too (9.1) — the Kingdom of God — to all people who would or could hear.

John the Baptist's function had been to point to this man who expressed in himself God's personal message. This message was to be identified and understood, according to Luke, by contrasting it with that of John the Baptist himself whose message was simply an exhortation to repentance for fear of the consequences of ignoring it. He had no news of the love of God or of anyone else — only of fear of God's anger and punishment.

11

THREE

Teachings and Signs

In the first five and a half chapters (as we have them) of his Gospel St Luke gives his readers his unique arrangement of the stories which narrate and connect the conception, birth and public appearance of John son of Zechariah and Jesus son of Mary. He shows much of this in parallel and intertwined conversations and events. He then makes John disappear and Jesus blossom, opening his public ministry with a startling appearance in the synagogue of his home town, immediately evoking both admiration and offence, so that some men responded to his call to follow him and some tried to do away with him. Both reactions were reinforced by subsequent very public actions and pronouncements. The authorities were horrified, while the crowds grew and followed him to listen, to watch and to bring him their sick whom he was able to heal. Power was in him and went out from him. It was a man thought to be demented who called him "the Holy One of God," yet it is quite clear that this is the revelation that Luke himself wishes to convey.

We read in these first chapters that one of the things that drew the crowds was the teaching of Jesus, but just what he taught is not mentioned until chapter 6.30: "Then turning to his disciples he began to speak . . ." The notable exception is the "parable" at the end of chapter 5 about the unwisdom of new cloth patching an old cloak, and of new wine in old wine-skins: fresh skins for new wine; and the old wine is preferred to new! Many parables come later, but after more encounters — and after the teaching about the character that his disciples are to aim at.

In this teaching there are many surprising commands, and the surprise of them is surely the main reason they were remembered and recorded. They are clear and pithy exhortations which must often have been something different to accepted morality, just as they are, very largely, in our time. But their central object is that "you will be sons of the Most High": in other words, a disciple's character should reflect the character of God himself. "You must love your enemies . . . Be compassionate as your Father is compassionate."

Here we come to the core of the "good news" — the news that this is what God is like. This is the Gospel of Jesus: love is his word for it, and his life is its practical expression; the purpose of Luke is to convey this in his writing. "A pupil is not (required to be) superior to his teacher." Jesus's disciples are not called to be better than God, kinder or more compassionate – of course not – but the heights to which they are called are such that they may reflect God. The notable and surprising thing is that God is kind and compassionate to everyone, even his "enemies"; that he does not pass judgement or condemn; that he acquits and gives freely. His disciples are likewise to be kind to the ungrateful and the wicked, like "your Father". Similarly, in chapter 17.3,4, the apparently unlimited ("seven times a day") forgiveness required towards "your brother" cannot be more generous than that of their Father. God, then, is himself the unlimited giver and forgiver.

In chapter 7 there come the stories of four surprising events, in which Jesus says and does highly significant things. At this point all that has been narrated so far seems to come to a climax and to be illustrated in the last of the four.

First (verses 1-10), Jesus at Capernaum is told of the serious illness of a Roman centurion's servant; the centurion, who is a foreigner and a representative of the occupying forces, sends some Jewish elders to Jesus, who describe the centurion as a friend of their nation and worthy of his help in saving the servant's life. More friends come to meet Jesus with the message that he need "only say the word" for healing to take place, for the centurion is familiar with words of authority. Jesus says publicly that he has not met faith like this anywhere in Israel.

14

The servant is found to be in good health when the messengers return to the house.

Secondly (verses 11-17), at Nain Jesus in a large crowd meets a funeral. He says "Weep no more" to the dead man's widowed mother. At his command the dead man sits up and speaks, and Jesus gives him back to his mother. The crowd, in awe and praise, recognise that there is a prophet among them who is showing God's care for his people.

Thirdly (verses 18-30), John the Baptist, in prison, is told of all this by his disciples and sends two of them to Jesus with the question "Are you the one who is to come . .?" Whereupon Jesus publicly cures many more sufferers, and tells John's disciples to report what they have heard and seen, perhaps especially that the poor are hearing the good news. Are these signs of the Messiah? Is the prophecy of Isaiah chapter 61 being fulfilled? Would John recall Jesus in the Nazareth synagogue and his announcement then? Jesus quotes more scripture and relates it to John and to God's special messenger: "Here is my herald . . . he will prepare your way."

The people indeed praised God, again, but the Pharisees and lawyers, having by contrast refused John's baptism, "rejected God's purpose for themselves"; they failed to appreciate what Luke sees as a clear demonstration in Jesus of the nature and activity of God whose compassion is shown to know no bounds and to have no conditions − the message and the messenger whose coming John had tried to prepare them for.

This is John's final appearance in Luke; he and his message are written out of the story of Jesus, for he has accomplished just what he was commissioned to do — to point us away from himself and his background, and towards the one who is mightier than he; Luke records his beheading by Herod in chapter 9.9.

Now, in chapter 7.36-50, comes one of the Gospel's most vivid and significant stories. One of the Pharisees has invited Jesus to eat with him at his house; a woman of "an immoral life", having heard of this, comes in with a flask of ointment. She wets his feet with tears, wipes them with her hair, then kisses and anoints them. In response to his host's objections, Jesus addresses him, Simon, with a parable about two debtors who were each let off by their money-lender. Replying to Jesus, Simon acknowledges that the one who was let off most would love him most. This woman was showing great love (and greater than Simon's), proving "that her many sins have been forgiven" (7.47). The Greek verb is in the perfect indicative passive tense, as also at 5.20, — page 11 above — her sins have (already) been taken away. The Jerusalem Bible translation is "her sins must have been taken away". Jesus does not say that she is forgiven much because she has loved much; nor was this the meaning conveyed in the story of the debtors.

16

She behaved as she did, not in order to be forgiven or to win love, but to show her deep gratitude and love for being already forgiven. Somehow she knew this — she had seen and heard Jesus in the previous days. Here Luke, in telling her story, proclaims the heart of the good news. He rounds off with Jesus's words of confirmation and strength (7.48) ''Your sins have been forgiven [same word] . . . Your faith has saved you . . .''

It must be significant that Luke has also used this verb in the same perfect tense in his telling of Jesus speaking to the palsied man brought to him through the roof (5.20), changing the tense of the verb in his editing of Mark's account (2.5), if we assume Mark is earlier, where the verb is in the present, as it also is in Matthew: ''are forgiven'' in Mark becoming ''have been forgiven'' in Luke in both instances.

This is surely the only way in which the parable about the debtors can be relevant and important in the situation that Jesus faced. Translations have missed the point, for example the Authorised Version and the NEB, and many commentators have confused and been confused by it, believing that a contradiction must be accepted as the solution to a perceived puzzle.

This passage was chosen as the alternative Gospel for reading on St Luke's Day in the proposed 1928 Prayer Book revision (not in BCP or ASB). This suggests that it must then have been recognised as the centre of gravity of the teaching of Jesus in St Luke's Gospel, even though its full meaning is not made clear in the Prayer Book version.*

Here is the climax of the section of Luke which begins (at chapter 4.14) with Jesus opening his public ministry, quoting from Isaiah and saying "Today in your very hearing this text has come true." Now Luke gives us the picture of someone who recognises and accepts it, and in an act of responding love fearlessly acknowledges herself to be accepted, loved and forgiven by God, and so made whole, saved, as she welcomes and marvels at it in an act of worship — knowing herself to be all unworthy in her own eyes and in the eyes of the world. (The world makes different assessments and different demands for the reconciliation of offenders!)

All this is now further illustrated by signs and words in chapter eight and the following chapters, as Jesus goes with the Twelve and others from town to town proclaiming the good news of the kingdom of God in parables and by direct teaching, often in

* According to the Church Assembly, House of Bishops, Minutes of Proceedings of the Committee on Prayer Book Revision, for January 13 1926, the Bishop of Chichester, Dr W O Burrows, moved that an alternative Gospel for St Luke's Day be provided. This was carried 25-3; and he himself suggested Luke 7.36-50: carried 19-7 by the relevant Members-in-Charge group of which he was Chairman.

synagogues, on the Sabbath, to crowds, to "tax gatherers and other bad characters", and to the Pharisees. By contrast, John the Baptist had required the people to come to him, static, by the Jordan.

Chapter 15 has three parables which Jesus addresses to those who complain that he welcomes sinners and eats with them. The wayward sheep and the lost coin are searched for until they are found by their shepherd and owner, and their findings are celebrated with public rejoicing − a picture of the joy in the heart of God at the repentance of a sinner. Then follows the great parable of the prodigal son (or of the generous father) in which all this is wonderfully portrayed in story form. We note that the father had already forgiven his son before the son got back to him, before he "confessed" to him, when "he was still a long way off". The son came home trustingly, to receive the benefit of this forgiveness, to be made alive again in his father's household.

Jesus, then, was taking the message of God to the sick and the outcasts, to foreigners, to mourners, to the hard-hearted, even to the dead. It was the good news of the unearned and unconditional, indiscriminate and unbounded love of God.

God's love, compassion and forgiveness do not have to be pleaded for, worked for or earned by us: they are not conditional on any action or non-action on our part. They are not dependant on our request, confession, penitence or faith, nor even given with the provision that we respond in any way. They are there as a permanent fact of life, for us to receive and accept, so that his saving health may be enjoyed. To trust and believe this is the channel required for our receiving the benefits of God's grace for newness of life.

And this has always been so, though mankind, even "the people of God", like John the Baptist, have not realised or recognised this. We are, perhaps, so conscious of our failings — which we particularly notice in other people; we require and demand recompense from each other for real or imagined unkindnesses of various sorts; we find it so hard to forgive others. We therefore find it hard to imagine how God, the God who is justice, can forgive without demanding his pound of flesh, our apology with promise of amendment. Even the Church, trying to proclaim him, has erected ecclesiastical hurdles or ritual hoops for people to negotiate before it proclaims sin forgiven in God's name.

But God is not in this demanding. The truth is, according to the Gospel, the almost unbelievable generosity of God from the beginning and to eternity — the generosity which caused and was demonstrated in the taking of flesh by God himself in the person of Jesus of Nazareth, leading to its culmination in his death at the hands of those he loved. His cross is the shorthand summary and sign of this message.

FOUR

Two Questions — and The Answer

From chapter 8 of Luke's Gospel we have the public words and actions of Jesus among the people as he went "from town to town and village to village, proclaiming the good news of the Kingdom of God." To this proclamation the people made their varying responses; these included the two big and natural questions which dominate the drama of this section and which Luke specifically gives us at the beginning and end of it.

First of all, the small band of disciples are in the boat with Jesus in a storm on the lake; as wind and waves obey his command and all becomes calm, they say among themselves in fear and astonishment, "Who can this be?" By way of indirect answer there comes, in the following scene, the cry of the demented man as Jesus was ordering out the unclean spirit, "What do you want with me, Jesus Son of the Most High God?" The man, now calm, is sent home by Jesus: "Tell them everything that God has done for you" he tells him.

Then Herod hears what is happening through Jesus and his disciples, and asks "Who is this . . ?" It could not be John, the one who had previously caused him trouble, for "I beheaded him myself."

Jesus himself puts the same question to his disciples: "Who do the people say I am?" One of the old prophets come back to life is the best explanation they have heard. Then the great question: "Who do you say I am?" Peter answers "God's Messiah."

A week later Jesus takes Peter and two others up into the hills to pray, and out of the cloud of his transfiguration comes a voice, "This is my son, my chosen." Luke gives us everything that follows to read and study in the context of this declaration. There is the element of questioning, and of suspicion and enmity, in all the narrative of subsequent confrontations, till his enemies accost him and put the question another way: "Tell us by what authority you are acting like this; who gave you this authority?" But he will not spell it out for them, as if he would let the deeds speak for themselves, if they would only understand: an echo of his earlier reply to the messengers of John the Baptist.

Then, at last their prisoner, he is brought before the Jewish Council for their final crowning question: "Are you the Messiah? Are you the Son of God?" They thought he said Yes, and brought him to

22

Pilate, the Governor with Caesar's authority, who asked him, "Are you the King of the Jews?"

Luke then tells us that these questions were repeated in parallel torments at his crucifixion. The people and their rulers said, "If this is God's Messiah, his chosen, let him save himself." The soldiers joined in, "If you are the King of the Jews, save yourself!"

Who was he? What was the authority for his words and deeds? Each listener, each spectator, and now each reader, has the challenge of the questions to respond to. Is this the Son of God? Does he personify the God of Abraham and of Moses, of Amos and Hosea and Isaiah, of the Psalms and of the Wisdom literature? Is the spirit of the continuing Father of the generations of Israelites to be seen in him? Is he the very hope of mankind? Does he represent the character that is the most admirable for men and women to worship and to honour and to desire for themselves? Are we drawn to look at him as the source of saving health for all persons and nations? Do we want to say to him, "My Lord and my God"?

In what must be the starkest context in history for the facing of questions like this, Luke tells us of the two unknown outcasts who make their respective declarations: one desperate and apparently scornfully rejecting him with "Are you not the Messiah? Save yourself and us." The other, similarly desperate but acknowledging the justice of the price he was paying for his misdeeds, against all human odds trustingly turns at least his mind to his dying "innocent" companion: "Jesus, remember me when you come to your throne — your royal power."

Only faith could see any sign of royalty or power there — faith that behind or in this man there was something stronger than all the power which had brought him to this point. If that was true, it was worth casting oneself on to it and on to him who personified it, and so make him one's Lord.

In his quotation of Jesus's last loud self-committing cry, Luke reminds us of the first words of Jesus that he quoted. To the same Father, in whose house he was found as a twelve-year-old boy declaring that he must learn his Father's business, he finally commits his spirit about twenty years on.

A watching centurion, a man who was himself under orders and who recognised loyalty to a real and known authority, at least glimpses the hidden truth as he gives his answer to these questions: "Beyond all doubt this man was innocent." Luke evidently desires us to understand that the centurion had heard the two calls from the cross: "Father, forgive . . ." and "Father, into your hands . . .": simple cries but of enormous power. He was clearly addressing his God at critical moments, and doing so in the total trust and closest intimacy of a perfect relationship. God, the Most High, was for him not so great and mysterious as to be quite unapproachable and unknowable, nor was he one who inspired only

24

awe for his fearful justice; he was the caring and loving Father whom the ancient Jewish prophets had proclaimed and whom Jesus had faithfully portrayed. The Son possessed the authority of his Father and the Father of all human life. He was the Messiah dying for the truth that this is what all his life had demonstrated.

Luke ends his Gospel with the great dramatic vindication of all that has gone before, to balance the close of his work with its opening. Angels are brought back — two men in dazzling garments in the otherwise empty tomb are seen by the women who have come to anoint their master's body. With just the reflection of the brilliant light of the wholly divine that men and women can stand, they say what no-one could dare to invent or even imagine to be true. "Why search among the dead for one who lives?" the men asked. "He is not here: he has been raised." The message had to overcome every natural resistance in his disciples: surprise, for it was unprecedented; fear — they were terrified; disbelief, for it "appeared to them to be nonsense;" and the constraints of the physical world were no hindrance.

Neither were they a hindrance in the curiously comparable narration by Luke of the events surrounding his birth. Being "still a virgin", Mary "was deeply troubled" by Gabriel's message; and the shepherds had been "terror-stricken" by the angel who stood before them and when "the splendour of the Lord shone round them." Mary was calmed with

"Do not be afraid, Mary", and was promised great wonders. Similarly the angel said to the shepherds, "Do not be afraid", and told them that "there is great joy coming to the whole people". Having seen the baby lying in the manger, as the shepherds had said, they recounted what they had been told about this child; and all were astonished at what the shepherds said. Then on the Resurrection morning the angels in the tomb calmed the terrified women, and later Jesus himself, "standing among them", when the Emmaus pair returned to the eleven in Jerusalem, pacified them with "Why are you so perturbed? . . . It is I myself." The final sentence of the Gospel seems to fulfil the first promise; for, after the risen Jesus had parted from them with his blessing, the witnesses "returned to Jerusalem with great joy". The shepherds prefigured the Apostles whose command and future work it was to take the good news to all nations.

Once again the initiative and will of God had won over the hearts and minds of faithful people. The Son of God was alive − risen from the dead, for his death and burial had unquestionably been witnessed by them three days previously. This was no mere apparition, for he was ready to be touched, and he ate and conversed with them. Nor was his dead body to be found in the tomb or anywhere else, though everyone must have had a natural interest in discovering it.

Here surely was vindication, authentication, by the most high and most holy God that this was his Messiah, his chosen, and that all the sayings of Jesus about the Father, and all the prayers he had addressed to him, were true and accepted. The men and women who had accompanied him from Galilee were the witnesses, says Luke, and he truly bore the title "Son of God" that the angel Gabriel had foretold to his mother.

Of course, as he commanded, the message about him must go to the whole world, beginning from Jerusalem within whose walls and environs all this had happened. For this was the message of God who by definition is the creating and living Spirit for all mankind by whom he may be known in the depth of their consciousness and who may then respond to the revelation of his love.

This was indeed the core of the proclamation of the Apostles in the following months and years, as Luke gives us in his continuing work, The Acts. The gospel of Jesus was no private vision or experience to be kept by a few, or with relevance limited to certain types or situations. As Simeon had said as he received him, a week old, in the temple, he was the "light that will be a revelation to the heathen, and glory to thy people Israel."

FIVE

The Effects

What then was effected by Jesus? What did God's incarnation and the life and death of Jesus do? It has often been said, (started by St Paul, the Pharisee?) as an interpretation of this great event, that a change was made in the fundamental relationship between God and mankind. Our liturgies and doctrinal formularies are full of phrases such as "the redemption of the world by our Lord Jesus Christ", and he himself is worshipped as our redeemer — which implies, indeed proclaims, that such a change was made: that God regards mankind now in a different way since the death of Jesus, and that his death enabled this change to be made. This means that there has been a change in the mind of God, in his outlook, in his side of the relationship. This means a change in the way real things are, in the fundamentals.

But how can we accept this? Has not God always been the same; is he not by definition unchangeable forever? God of the Old Testament is

28

surely also God of the New who has himself not changed or been changed. Rather surely it is mankind's perception that may have changed because it is incomplete, according to God's self-revelation and our reception: varied through the centuries and round the world.

The Christian message − like its messenger − did not inaugurate a fundamentally new situation. God is and always has been loving and forgiving towards all people; if he had not been so there would have been no incarnation, no Jesus. This was and is the message of the Old Testament prophets and of the interpreters of the events of Jewish history; it is the main theme of the Psalms through and in which the Jewish worshippers have expressed their understanding of the basis of the relationship between God and themselves and the world in general. These Psalms the Christian Church has naturally incorporated into its own worship.

God, of the Old and the New Testaments, loves his people and is forgiving, not because they are faithful or obedient (though he does love their obedience when it happens) but even when they are not, even when they deliberately rebel. His love for them is not dependant on their showing love for him. The prophets are constantly seeking to excite the people's love for and obedience to God as a response to God's love for them and his calling of them to himself; for this is the way their relationship may be complete and fruitful, and they themselves be saved. God forgives their sin, much as he hates it for it is a turning away from him. He forgives, over and over again, for he loves so much, in spite of their continual back-sliding, and he continuously calls them to respond not out of fear of him but of love for his love. This is the everlasting truth which Jesus encapsulates and incarnates in his person and his message, and which St John proclaims in his letter — that we love because he first loved us.

Should we not therefore free ourselves from the idea of redemption, leaving it in the particular Old Testament context of the temple sacrifices which applied in the later centuries before Christ? If so, we can cease all the difficult discussion as to whom and for what purpose the redemption price was or is to be made in the Christian era; discussions which are only relevant to and appreciated by those who grasp the Jewish sacrificial ideas. We can in fact leave them with John the Baptist who was born into the priestly system, whose baptism was to signify repentance and purification before God, and who pointed to the One who, greater than he, would baptise with the very Spirit of God, heralding forgiveness, as we have noted, without a price. John's death signalled the death of that system, its irrelevance, and its divergence from the revelation of God in the prophetic history of Israel; John, son of Zechariah, was the herald of the true revelation in the person of Jesus, son of Mary, the prophet from Nazareth in Galilee.

The angels at Bethlehem gave the world the theme of the message which the incarnation, the whole story of Jesus, proclaims: God's goodwill towards mankind, and peace to his people on earth. This goodwill was already there; the baby lying in the manger was the demonstration. God did not need the life or death of Jesus Christ to make it possible for him to forgive; but mankind needs it to appreciate the truth and the depth of the eternal love which forgives. "Christ died for us while we were yet sinners, and that is God's own proof of his love towards us" wrote St Paul — Romans 5.8. His death demonstrated more convincingly than any prophet's words what is in the heart of God eternally for all mankind.

The agony and the fearfulness involved in Jesus's crucifixion also contain a message for us about the depth of God's concern for us and his pain at our sin, as he shares our pains and suffers the consequences of our sin. Correspondingly, they speak about the vital need for mankind to know and be convinced of his forgiveness and to accept it — the forgiveness that is at the heart of God's creation, mysterious and waiting to be discovered and experienced.

The Church's message — the really good news — is to sinners: not "You can be forgiven by God if you believe and repent, if you do or resolve to do this or that," but "God has already forgiven you

31

because he loves you; without your asking, or deserving, or even knowing, you are forgiven. Contemplate the person and the cross of Jesus; there is the sign. Respond by repentance, and so know life and freedom.''

This is essentially the same as the message of the Old Testament prophets who proclaimed the undiminished love of God for his people, and the call for their repentance as a response, thus completing the intimate relationship, the covenant, which was initiated by God for their benefit. The Jews to whom Jesus spoke were nurtured on these scriptures; they knew repentance was vital, and Jesus stressed that it still was. He said he had come ''to call sinners to repentance'' (5.32); and ''unless you repent you will come to the same end'' as those who perished (13.5). Luke writes in chapter 11 that Jesus recalled the people of Nineveh, their predecessors, who repented at the preaching of Jonah, and ''what is here is greater than Jonah''. He warned them in parables of the possibility of their being excluded from the presence of God in his Kingdom by their failure to repent in the face of God's graciousness towards them: 10.13, 13.23-24, 14.15-24. He spoke of his longing to gather the people of Jerusalem to him, but ''you would not let me.'' And ''alas'' for the Pharisees and the lawyers who are themselves blind to the love of God for people and so obscure it in their teaching. He includes some fearful warnings: 11.51, 12.5 and 46.

But the core of St Luke's Gospel is the words and actions of Jesus proclaiming God and his forgiving love.

"Father, forgive them" was Jesus's prayer (Luke 23.34 — and only in Luke) for his crucifiers, though there is no suggestion that they were penitent. According to St Luke, this was spoken by Jesus apparently for the soldiers as representatives of the whole sinning world. "They do not know what they are doing" he said.

This must be one of the most amazing sayings recorded of Jesus. Luke has told us that many people were healed and forgiven without penitence or love or faith on their part. Here at the climax of Jesus's life — in fact his death — his parting words are a call for the father's forgiveness for those who were actually killing him. They were ignorant, helpless, under orders, virtually mindless, loveless: and forgivable.

It is the same message as in Luke 1-7, though in starker and summary terms. Luke, it seems, is desperate to get his understanding of the message of God in Jesus across to Theophilus and others, in his "portrait" of God as revealed by Jesus. This is the voice of God speaking for the world of people who are unworthy to face the good God; they are therefore afraid of him and of the truth, and so turn their back or rebel against him, or live with guilty fears.

This is God expressing himself outloud,

revealing his mind to mankind. As the angel said to the shepherds: "Do not be afraid; I have good news for you: there is great joy coming to the whole people."

Must we not beware of separating Jesus and the Father into two distinct "people"? If we do so at this point, we could conceive the possibility of the Father responding to this plea of the Son in one of the following ways:

(a) Yes, I will forgive them since you ask me and plead with me with your life and your last breath. (If you had not I might not have done so); or

(b) Yes, now I can forgive them because you have offered yourself as a perfect sacrifice to me as propitiation for all their misdoings; or

(c) No, I will not, in spite of your plea.

None of these seem to ring true as possibilities. Yet do not traditional and orthodox interpretations of the crucifixion suggest or require the responses (a) or (b)?

Instead, can we not say that this is God talking to himself as Jesus reveals the divine mind, "a soliloquy in the heart of God", and mankind has the amazing privilege of overhearing it? [I owe that phrase to Bishop Kenneth Cragg, in a lecture].

34

Here, in the crucifixion of Jesus of Nazareth, is a demonstration, with a verbal accompaniment, of the love of God "who first loved us". The cross is the measure of that love which is expressed in forgiveness, unconditional, indiscriminate, universal — the love in the heart of the Creator and so at the heart of creation: love given to his creatures who are made in his image so that they are able to reflect him.

The incarnation, including the crucifixion, of Jesus has not changed God's mind — that is impossible. Surely it has not in some mysterious way enabled God to forgive when previously he could not. Rather it has proclaimed forgiveness in and among sinning humanity in a way that anyone can see and appreciate, for it has been shown in the person of a human being sent from and appointed by God, who bears God's own message: the faithful Son who reflects the nature of his Father.

It must also be significant that in each case where Jesus is recorded in the Gospels as proclaiming the forgiveness of sin, viz: Luke 5.20 (Mark 2.5, Matthew 9.2) and Luke 7.48, it is always in the passive: "Your sins have been (or are) forgiven"; never "I forgive . . ." The lawyers and Pharisees, mishearing or misunderstanding, complain each time: "Who is this that he can forgive sins? Who but God alone . . ?" Correct! Here is Luke saying, through the words and in the person of Jesus, that God himself has done precisely that.

The response which is called for from the forgiven is simply love, inspired by the Spirit of God who is himself limitless love and for whose portrait we are all indebted to St Luke.

At the end of his Gospel it is perhaps surprising to find Luke writing that the risen Lord Jesus addressed the eleven Apostles and sent them out with his message: ''This is what is written: that the Messiah is to suffer death and to rise from the dead on the third day, and that in his name repentance bringing the forgiveness of sins is to be proclaimed to all nations. Begin from Jerusalem; it is you who are the witnesses to it all.''

This may not seem to be a fair summary of the gospel of Jesus as proclaimed by St Luke, though this, the final recorded words of Jesus, would be a fitting place for such a summary.

''Repentance bringing the forgiveness of sins'' is not the main theme of St Luke's work, nor of the preaching of Jesus in it, and this phrase does not appear elsewhere in the Gospel. It is therefore curious that this could seem to be the message that St Luke believed Jesus to commission his Apostles to proclaim. The emphasis in the Gospel is, as we have seen, that repentance is called for as a response to the knowledge of God's initiative of loving forgiveness and not as a necessary condition of it.

We may wonder how this phrase got into the Gospel at this point. There are echoes of it in what is generally regarded as St Luke's second book, The Acts of the Apostles. For example:

Acts 2.38 — "Repent," said Peter [to the Jewish crowd on the Day of Pentecost], "repent and be baptised, every one of you, in the name of Jesus the Messiah for the forgiveness of sins; and you will receive the gift of the Holy Spirit. For the promise is to you, and to your children, and to all who are far away, everyone whom the Lord may call."

Acts 3.18 — Peter [to the men of Israel] ". . . this is how God fulfilled what he had foretold in the utterances of all the prophets: that his Messiah should suffer. Repent then and turn to God, so that your sins may be wiped out."

Acts 5.30 — Peter replied [to the high priest] for himself and the Apostles: ". . . the God of our fathers raised up Jesus whom you had done to death . . . He it is whom God has exalted with his own right hand as leader and saviour, to grant Israel repentance and forgiveness of sins."

Acts 10.39,43 — Peter [to Cornelius and companions at Caesarea]: "(Jesus) was put to death . . . but God raised him to life on the third day . . . It is to him that all the prophets testify, declaring that everyone who trusts in him receives forgiveness of sins through his name."

Act 11.18 — [the Holy Spirit having come

37

upon all who heard the above address, and Peter relating it to the Apostles] (The Apostles) gave praise to God and said, "This means that God has granted life-giving repentance to the gentiles also."

Each of the passages quoted seems to suggest that forgiveness comes following repentance. Further, each passage is part of an address by Peter to gatherings of Jews, and is in the context of a mention of the shamefulness of the crucifixion of Jesus, and in the last two of his resurrection. The last one is the simple declaration which is the key and climax to them all − gentiles as well as Jews were within the orbit of the love of God.

The other mentions of repentance in Acts are: (8.22) Peter fiercely urges Simon the magician to "repent of this wickedness and pray the Lord to forgive you for imagining such a thing", that is, that he could buy from Peter and John their power to bestow the Holy Spirit through the laying on of hands; and (17.30 and 20.21) Paul is twice quoted in his insistance on God's behalf that all mankind, Jews and gentiles alike, should repent and trust in the Lord Jesus.

While the message of "repentance bringing forgiveness of sins" is not the centre of gravity of Luke's Gospel and is therefore not a fair summary of it, the fact that it is to be proclaimed by the Apostles beyond the boundaries of Judaism is a major change for the Jews and a shock to them.

38

". . . to all nations . . ." in Luke 24.47 is probably the real point of emphasis in this report of Jesus's parting words; and it is taken up later by Peter and the young Church as they discover and realise it. Forgiveness by God for themselves was not a new idea for the Jews — their scriptures, our Old Testament, are full of it — but that it should be a gift for non-Jews was news indeed, in so far as they had forgotten the ancient promise and revelation to Abraham, and the scriptural echoes of it through the centuries. St Luke points out that Jesus said "This is . . . what is written."

Repentance was therefore also available for gentiles, making it possible for them to share with Jews the fullness of the grace of God and of newness of life. Barriers were indeed broken down as St Paul also proclaimed. There really was no distinction between Jew and gentile. God is one, and all are one in God.

We are reminded of John the Baptist's quotation of the prophecy of Isaiah chapter 40. It is recorded in all four Gospels, but Luke (3.4-6) gives us a fuller version than do the others. He alone quotes the whole section down to the line ". . . and all mankind (flesh) shall see God's deliverance." Jesus refers (4.24-27) to the widow at Sarepta and Naaman the Syrian receiving visits, with food and healing, from the prophets Elijah and Elisha, rather than Israelites. And we remember the announcement by the angels at the birth of Jesus that "there is great joy coming to the whole (or, all the) people" through the child who is, in Simeon's prophecy, the "deliverance which God has made ready in full view of all the nations: a light that will be a revelation to the heathen, and glory to thy people Israel" (2.31,32).

So here, in the Gospel of Luke and in Acts, is the universal message of the one God to all people, Jews and gentiles, religious and pagan, Christians and Muslims . . .: the God and Creator of all mankind, addressing himself to all his creatures with whom he desires to share his nature, so that they may all receive his life in full measure, knowing and sharing his love.

Love is his nature, and forgiving love is his command. This is how the world of people in all their relationships is intended and designed to work: this is how they are called to live, and this is the yardstick against which they are judged. The message is delivered by God himself through his chosen messenger who faithfully reflects him in his life of love. It is not sectarian doctrine for a few, but creation truth for all.

"Believe it, repent, and live it!"

SIX

Some Consequences

From this study of St Luke's "portrait" of Jesus in his Gospel there arise some consequences for our understanding and belief which should be reflected in our doctrine and our worship as expressed in our public liturgy.

A

Luke seems to proclaim that
  i   God loves, and therefore
 ii   God forgives:
iii   People are called upon to repent as a
       response, and
 iv   to love God and their neighbour: the two
       great commandments.

All this is shown by the words and actions of Jesus and of those people whom Luke brings into his story. This follows on from and is consistent with the proclamations of the Old Testament prophets. Chapters 1 to 7 "say" all this, and a comparison and a contrast is made with John the Baptist. The message of Jesus was true to that of the prophets (7.22) and John's was a mistaken variation of it. Jesus's was surprising, and therefore hard to receive, especially by the hard-headed Pharisees and ecclesiastics who anyway had not accepted John either (7.30). John's message, by contrast, was rather ordinary and sounded sensible and was therefore more acceptable.

But much of our teaching and our liturgy has it differently: viz.

i   People are to hear God's commands, be convinced, then
ii   Repent.
iii   God the father forgives penitent believers through Christ as
iv   they resolve and are enabled to lead godly lives.

This is more like John the Baptist's message than Jesus's. We seem to say that Jesus has enabled God to forgive, or that he has made it possible for God's forgiveness to be received: he, the Son, is therefore the saviour/redeemer in his mediation with the Father for his disciples. This suggests that the kind Son propitiates the angry Father and so alters the situation: God's mind is changed as far as mankind is concerned and forgiveness is possible for the first time.

We can recall what we actually say in church. At Morning and Evening Prayer the Minister pronounces that:

"Almighty God, the Father of our Lord Jesus Christ, . . . hath given power and commandment to his ministers to declare and pronounce to his people, being penitent, the absolution and remission of their sins: he pardoneth and absolveth all them that truly repent, and unfeignedly believe his holy gospel."

At the Communion, "Almighty God, our heavenly Father, who of his great mercy hath promised forgiveness of sins to all them that with hearty repentance and true faith turn unto him, have mercy upon you, pardon and deliver you . . ."

(The Book of Common Prayer)

The corresponding sections in the Alternative Service Book reduce the stated conditions for forgiveness:

"Almighty God, who forgives all who truly repent . . ." in Morning and Evening Prayer and in the Communion; the invitation to confession in the Communion, though, is: "Let us confess our sins, in penitence and faith . . ."

These conditions for forgiveness by God do not seem to be faithful reflections of the Gospel, in particular as told by St Luke. The phrases imply and emphasise the message of John son of Zechariah rather than that of Jesus, and are not a proclamation of unconditional love and forgiveness in the heart of God. They are not even faithful to the Old Testament where the same God is revealed, he whose prophets call people to love and worship: God who now, as then, draws his people to repentance, by his constant, indiscriminating love: he is the God of all mankind who is revealed, and whose mind is expressed, in the works, words and person of Jesus of Nazareth, son of Mary.

This is God whom the Church of Christ has the privilege and responsibility of proclaiming and of worshipping in words which must not mislead but, as faithfully as is humanly possible, should express its faith and its understanding of the good news which Jesus brings to the world. One must conclude that some adjustment in the liturgical pronouncements quoted above is necessary, as a matter of faithfulness to the Gospels, for the Church must not say that forgiveness by God is conditional on penitence or even on faith.

B

There is a further problem in the Eucharistic Prayers, or Prayer of Consecration, as we currently have it. For some reason, with its roots in history, the phrase "for the forgiveness of sins" is included in the recitation of Jesus's words at the blessing of the wine

44

during the Last Supper: and so it is very familiar to worshippers, coming as it does at the solemn climax of the drama of the service:

> "This is my blood of the new covenant which is shed for you and for many for the forgiveness of sins . . ."

The phrase is peculiar to St Matthew's Gospel; neither Mark nor Luke include it in their account, nor is it in St Paul's in 1 Corinthians 11. (Mat. 26.38; Mark 14.24; Luke 22.20). We may wonder why Matthew, alone, has it, and why Matthew's phrase is apparently invariably included in the liturgical recitation. Is it not the only instance in the Gospels in which forgiveness is directly linked to the death of Jesus?

Not to include it would be to use better authenticated versions of the event and of early Church practice; and it would remove a problem for us: for we should not then find it necessary to interpret the suffering and death of Jesus in a way which is not consistent with the main thrust of the evidence of the Gospels, and to do it at such a prominent and central point.

That phrase does of course fit in naturally with the doctrine of the BCP Consecration Prayer and in the third and fourth Eucharistic Prayers of the ASB, but is not needed in the simpler first and second of the latter.

We have no need to say — and St Luke does not suggest — that the suffering and death of Jesus happened in order that sin(s) might be forgiven, though this has of course been taught by theologians and adopted by hymn writers and other interpreters (following especially The Epistles to The Galatians and Hebrews): that now all sin could be, or has been, forgiven by God through the cross of Christ, and believers can receive that forgiveness by repentance, and that they can be actively involved in this act of redemption by partaking of the blood of Christ in the wine of the Eucharist: saying in effect that apart from the cross and faith in it, there is no forgiveness!

Rather, the paralysed man and the woman in Simon's house could receive forgiveness of their sins before the death of Jesus. Nor did Jesus himself need to wait to die before he could proclaim it. For neither did God require it to forgive.

The evidence of the Gospels is that the whole event of Jesus gives us the simplest, most dramatic and deepest demonstration and proclamation of the free and unbounded forgiving love in the heart of God, i.e. at the heart of creation, from the beginning and to all eternity — and so for all people; and that here in the Eucharist is the way for all of us, all unworthily, in love and humility to accept and receive the fact and the grace of it. This is surely what our liturgy must unequivocally proclaim.

C

We can also make a contribution to the discussion about infant baptism. This outward and visible sign proclaims God's forgiveness, and the inward and spiritual grace given to us, before one has a chance even to live at all. The baptised child enters the community which believes in, and intends to live by, the knowledge and the reality of forgiveness through the unconditional love of God for us all. This is therefore a fundamental sacrament of the Church.

For a minister, on behalf of the Church, to make the baptism of an infant conditional on parents' Church membership or attendance, or even on their belief, appears to be a denial of this Gospel, and to be an unintentional attempt to staunch the grace of God. The minister's responsibility is to teach those who desire the child's baptism, or to see that they are taught, and to accede to their request if it is maintained; thereby to show by word and this sacrament the true love and graciousness of God.

When infant baptism is occasionally and helpfully celebrated amongst the normal worshipping congregation at, especially, the Eucharist, then all join in this special sign and reminder of their entry into their common faith in God as revealed in Jesus.

This does of course imply the need for a revised service of baptism for infants (and for adults), in respect of the questions and answers, and of the homilies; and declarations as to the faith of parents should not be obligatory. The Church must not appear to be the sentry who has the password over entry into the Kingdom of God: rather the servant who opens the door with a welcome from the divine Father of all.

D

Probably the word most misleading to the general public, and yet for worshippers one which is in constant use in liturgy, is the adjective "almighty" when applied to God. It implies that God can do anything in his creation that he wishes independently of us, and in particular what seems to us, at least in our better moments, to need doing and that we cannot do. The evident fact that he does not, for instance, act directly to remove particular or general causes of suffering, and is yet said to be loving, calls into question any reasonableness for faith in him on Christian terms: as he plainly does not appear to be all-mighty, his very existence is in fundamental doubt. To allow the crucifixion of "his Son" seems to remove any justification for believing in an all-mighty being. Even if he exists at all, he cannot be properly described by what the words almighty and love seem to mean: unless, of course, we put the two words together as we really want to − but that takes some extra explanation!

'Almighty' is a word unknown to Luke or to any of the Gospels or Epistles, and would seem to be an unnecessary word to the Bible as a whole, except as a translation of a Hebrew title for the one true sovereign God as opposed to false gods or gods of other nations; at best it would encourage and inspire human awe. Even the creation myths do not set out to consider the overwhelming all-mightiness of God as a cardinal characteristic for his worshippers to acknowledge. Neither Old nor New Testament need this expression to focus on the loving Father of mankind.

Better, more faithful to the Bible, and a truer reflection certainly of the mind of St Luke, would be to address God in formal worship as "most high" (e.g. Luke 1.32 and 76) − or, as a more suitably rythmical substitute for "Almighty", "All Holy", "Holiest", or "Most Holy". Each of these would fit satisfactorily with "eternal" in Collects and other expressions used corporately, and would help to induce the supreme responses of loyalty and love, as well as of awe.

E

In his Gospel Luke desires his readers to see God in Jesus of Nazareth for whom God was Father; in Acts he tells of the Apostles being under the living guidance of the spirit of the risen Lord Jesus or of the Holy Spirit − terms which appear to be interchangeable and without distinguishing meaning; each clearly indicates the Spirit of God himself who dwells in the baptised disciples of Jesus; and it is he who spoke through the prophets of the Old Testament. So we have the great

49

distinguishing doctrine of the Christian Church — "three Persons in one God."

This Spirit is the often unrecognised thread who weaves throughout the scriptures and on whom the life of all God's people depends. He is the Spirit who has enlivened everyone and drawn them to the knowledge of God from Abraham onwards — the spirit of the one true God who is revealed in Jesus the Christ, son of Mary. He is the Spirit of God "almighty" — there is no other God — who may be thought of as original Creator because he upholds all that is. As the earliest Israelites tried to explain whom it was they worshipped and trusted, they therefore pictured God as the Creator.

But just as "almighty" is not a New Testament term for God, neither is "creator". Important as that attribute may be, it is not as significant to New Testament people as is the presence of the personal God. Indeed the term can be unhelpful as it tends to deflect one's attention to a past creation event which is unknowable — except maybe one day to advanced scientific discovery — and which is currently a huge puzzle; and it ties one's understanding of God to the continuing problems of the when and how and why of creation which are not the real concern of any Biblical writer. For the whole Bible is to do with the relationship between the spirit of the one God and the spirit of mankind. It is therefore more relevant and helpful to think of God as he who is continually creating, rather than he who at one time created. He *is*, and always was and ever shall be.

Our first and continuing experience of God is as spirit, his to ours and ours to his in response. This is the spirit of the one who is also "our Father in heaven", the generator of all that is; and his "nature is always to have mercy" towards us, as we see personified in his true Son.

So God is for us Spirit, and Father and his Son. He shows us these three faces or facets of his one substance, not three substances somehow unified. In this respect the word "Persons" can be a confusing translation; it is not the same as "people" as it often is in common parlance, though there is probably no better term: for we worship him, not them. He is creating, alive and present; he supports, inspires and guides; he is accepting, loving, and forgiving. He may be alarming at first, but in his presence is joy.

This is how Jesus was portrayed by Luke who was telling a story "on two levels", as Bishop John Robinson used to say, to illustrate the truth which is both material and spiritual, temporal and eternal, of earth and heaven, in order to tell people, of all times and traditions and types, of the one true God.

A PERSONAL POSTCRIPT

It was, I believe, a liberating experience for me to be chaplain at what was mainly a remand prison. It came comparatively late in my career and was a surprise appointment. I was there for four years and was in constant touch with men who were accused, and some of whom were convicted, of anti-social activities. The men, whether they had been found guilty or not, were treated or were generally regarded as likely to be guilty, and the primary and statutory duty of the prison authorities was drastically to curtail their precious liberty in case they were indeed so. The chaplains appeared to be involved in this also, but it was necessary to realise that the only excuse for the Church being officially there was to represent the God who made no judgements, gave no convictions, imposed no sentence; but who, while he totally knew and understood and cared, held out his arms to accept and love without qualification.

It was just not good enough to pronounce in Chapel to men whose knowledge of Christian faith and worship was minimal, or to say to them individually in so many words, "Almighty God who forgives all who truly repent, (if you do) have mercy upon you, pardon and deliver you from all your sins . . .": still less the Book of Common Prayer version.

Where was the truth in that, where the unique attraction of the one who will draw all men to himself? Where was the goodwill, good news and great joy, that will freely draw men to repentance and new life?

This was not just ministry to prisoners; it also vividly highlighted Christ's ministry generally, for it was ministry in God's name among contemporary society's outcasts, there through negligence or weakness — other people's or their own — or their own deliberate fault.

The Eucharist is, for all of us, the understandable demonstration in word and sacrament that somebody cares for each of us, and that anyone can receive, by his invitation and provision, the sign of that caring. Real love is unlimited, so forgiveness is granted to all, unconditionally, of whatever faith or none, by the true God of all.

We may, surely we must, legitimately and lawfully say: "God Most Holy forgives us all. He has mercy on us, and pardons and delivers us from all our sin. Lord, confirm and strengthen us in all goodness, and keep us in eternal life."

We may thankfully add, "For Jesus Christ's sake. Amen."

This we have learned, from good St Luke, of the love of God.

✝

BIBLIOGRAPHY

I am grateful to friendly and scholarly critics who have both encouraged and corrected me and whose continued comments will be valuable as well to me as to other learners from St Luke.

Amongst the very large number of works published on St Luke's Gospel and The Acts of the Apostles, I have referred, at least in part, to the following during the preparation of this treatise, for all of which I am grateful.

H Balmforth	The Gospel according to St Luke. The Clarendon Bible, Oxford, 1933
F F Bruce	The Book of The Acts. Revised ed. W B Eerdmans, Grand Rapids, Michigan, 1988
C B Caird	The Gospel according to St Luke. Pelican Books, 1963
J M Creed	The Gospel accoring to St Luke. Macmillan, 1930
J Drury	Tradition and Design in St Luke's Gospel. London, 1976
C K Evans	Saint Luke. SCM Pess, 1990
J A Findley	The Gospel according to St Luke: a Commentary. SCM, 1937
M D Goulder	Luke: A New Paradigm. JSOT Press, Sheffield, 1989
E Haenchen	The Acts of the Apostles. Oxford, 1971
J Jeremias	New Testament Theology. English translation, London and New York, 1971.
G W H Lampe	Peake's Commentary, chapter on St Luke's Gospel. Nelson, 1962
A R C Leaney	A Commentary on the Gospel according to St Luke. A & C Black, 2nd ed., 1966
J R Lumby	The Acts of the Apostles. Cambridge, 1907
R Maddox	The Purpose of Luke-Acts. Edinburgh, 1982
W Manson	The Gospel of Luke. *Moffat New Testament Commentaries*, Hodder and Stoughton, 1930
I H Marshall	The Gospel of Luke. *New International Greek Testament Commentary*, Paternoster Press, 1978
E Schweizer	The Good News according to Luke. *Trans.* D E Green. SPCK. 1984
Vincent Taylor	Forgiveness and Reconciliation. Macmillan, 1941

55

NOTE ON AUTHOR

After service in the RAF, Edmund Haviland
graduated from the University of Cambridge and then
attended Wells Theological College. He was ordained
deacon and priest in Southwark Cathedral. The author
has held appointments in south London, Derbyshire
and Kent. He served for one year in southern Africa
and four years as a prison chaplain.

Edmund Haviland is now retired and lives in Surrey.